Poetic Escape

My Freedom of Expression

Aaron Dillon

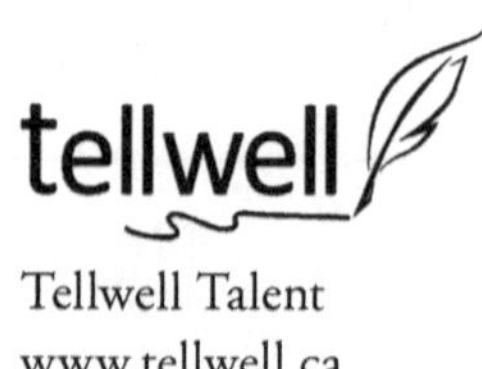

Tellwell Talent
www.tellwell.ca

ISBN
978-1-998482-77-1 (Paperback)

Table of Contents

Anxiety in Me

Can't remember the last time your life was fun.
All you're ever told is to talk to someone.
When all your friends want only to drink
Can't help but feel like your life is on the brink.
Lying in your bed trying not to cry
Praying it would disappear in the blink of an eye.
For they don't understand how it feels
Your head in a swirl, no longer at the wheel.

Months have passed since you've lost your crutch.
Whenever you were down, they'd help so much.
Never knew they were keeping you above ground.
Ever since their passing, your mind is rarely sound.
If you have someone's back, having yours is a must.
As it's quite difficult to gain your trust
Fearing, if you told someone that the word would spread.
Left to fly solo, battling these voices in your head.

Yeah, your mind's your one true enemy
Feeling like you're running out of energy.
Sick and tired of hearing it ain't that bad.
When you can't even talk to your mom or dad
Screamin' out you just wanna be free.
Crying out, "help me overpower, the anxiety in me".

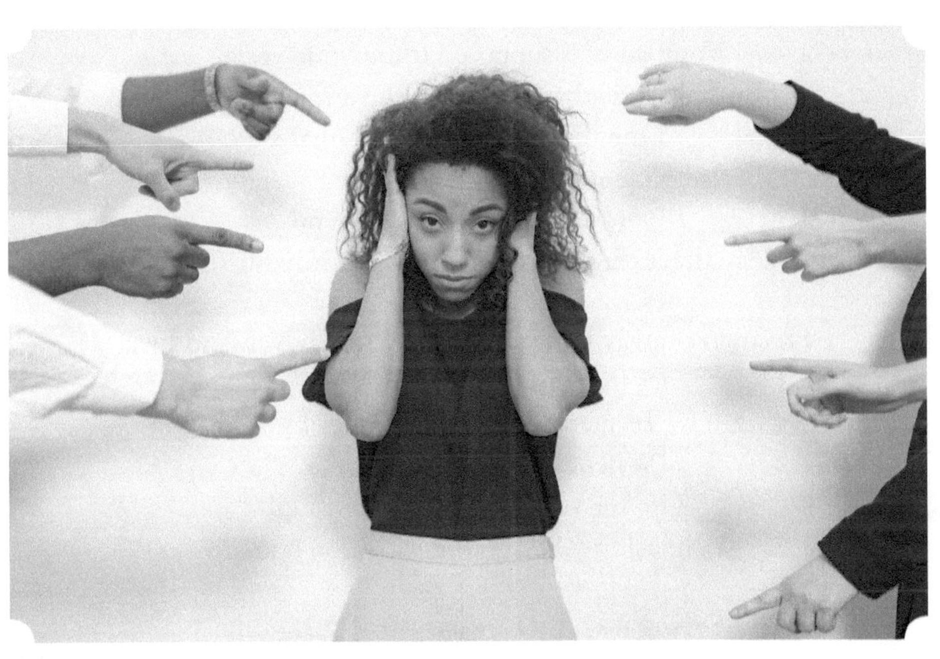

Body of Mine

Your body is supposed to be your vessel.
So why is it, that it deals with so much hassle.
One thing that you really hate.
Is being attacked, for not losing weight.
Everyone says that it's not abuse.
Why don't they try spending a day in your shoes?

From constantly being told that you'll never find love
For the fact that your clothes don't fit like a glove
To getting judgemental looks.
Whenever you get on the bus
Life for you has been quite tough.
Wondering when will enough be enough.

Seeing it constantly, boys and girls alike
Told to walk more or even to ride a bike.
These comments for some, into depression it sends.
Always telling your friends that
"I really miss the time, that I could feel
comfortable in this body of mine".

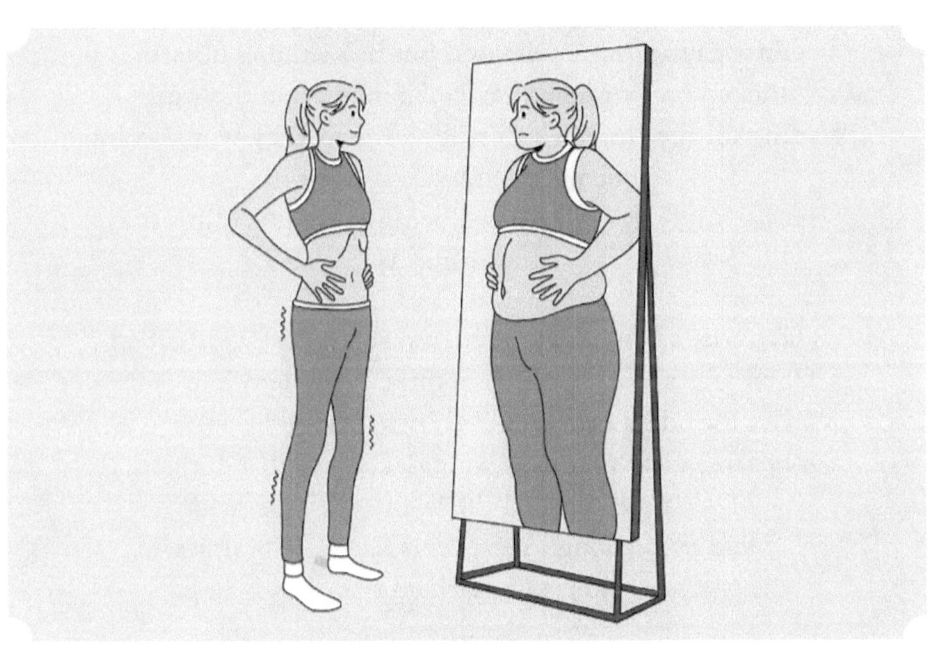

Colour Blind

First day at his new school, but he's finding it hard.
Picked on by other kids, called names on the yard.
Waiting for the final bell to ring, for tears they would bring.
All he ever wanted was to fit in,
But he wasn't given a chance because the hue of his skin.
[Insert line 1]

There was a noise complaint, and the police were called,
Upon arrival they realised, a mixed couple was at fault.
Both had bruises and things seemed hectic,
It became clear that they were dealing with a domestic.
They both recalled the events they claimed,
And even though her events had a lot of holes,
It was her coloured boyfriend that they blamed.
Evidence was clear, but they didn't care.
Incidents like this show us, the judicial system isn't fair.
[Insert line 1]

Her boss was leaving, so he would be promoting.
The staff he said they'd be the ones voting.
She's there the longest and her numbers are the best.
Her work rate is high, much higher than the rest.
Her colleagues said that she'd be serving,
So, everyone was shocked when the position
was given to someone undeserving.

She couldn't believe it, gone was her relief,
When she asked her boss why, he replied with "your beliefs".
[Insert line 2]

Line 1) Why can't they just look inside themselves, and try their best to find, that place in their hearts that is forever colour blind.

Line 2) I'm begging you, please look deep inside yourself, and search for that golden place in your mind which will remain forever colour blind.

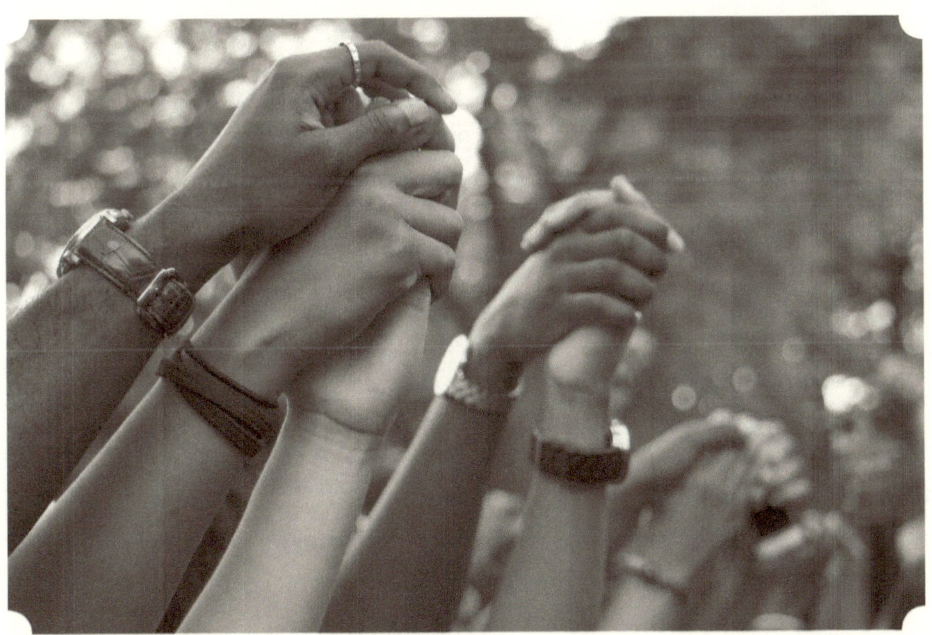

Fairy-tale Ending

His love is in a coma, fading slowly.
And everyone knows she'd be dearly missed,
As she lay there peacefully it was her lips that he kissed
She opened her eyes and smiled with glee.
His very own Sleeping Beauty.

Cold nights spent on the streets.
With little or nothing to eat
Searching for the warmest/safest place to sleep
Dreaming of shelter, like the giant shoe or palace of ice
Because God knew that anything would suffice.

Many crave love, whereas others need some.
Spent many sleepless nights, hoping for what was about to come.
She's found her ebony to her ivory.
Love at first sight, she had finally gotten her Cinderella Story.

Slitting her wrists, for she's never felt bliss.
Sister pleaded for her not to make her life a miss.
With this encouragement, she decided there was no more self-harming.
Opened up and found her own Prince Charming

Many still hope that he's listening to the prayers they're sending.
Waiting, wishing, and dreaming that they to
Can have their very own Fairy-tale Ending.

Freedom Fighters

The internet is a supposed safe haven,
Yet so many still cry out for savin'.
I've laid witness to it being a bullying realm,
Don't believe me? Do you remember Ask.FM.

Friends are supposed to support you through
tough times and be good mates,
It's when you're down that you'll spot the real from the fakes.
You would support them, give them your undivided attention.
But when the shoes on the other foot you get little mention.

Mental Health, a real villain to youth mainly
Many have fallen, ignored when they cried out "save me".
Lots still suffer with that sinking feeling,
Wondering, "Why is it that I feel six feet
deep, but I'm still breathing?"

Some However, had the support they needed to live on
And it's those people who encourage those suffering to stay strong.
They're no Bear Grylls, but they're born survivors.
Dealt with depression, no need to wave your lighters.
They're standing side by side as Freedom Fighters.

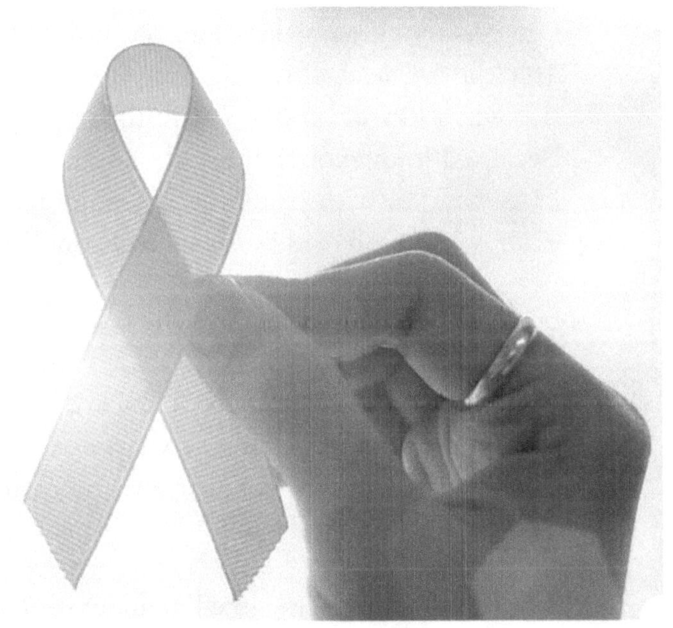

Guardian Angel

Life gets me down from time, and It's hard to cope,
To clear my head, I'd go for a walk.
But when I speak to you, I gain the hope.
Because I know you're listening, and it's easier to talk.
For when I'm with you I'm much more faithful
Yeah, when God made you, he made my Guardian Angel

Lying in bed and I'm feeling weak.
Try to talk to my parents, but always ends in strife!
How does texting you make it feel less bleak?
Every time we talk, I get a new lease on life.
For when I'm around you, life feels more graceful.
Yeah, when God made you, he made my Guardian Angel

From constantly feeling like I'm under immense pressure.
To now feeling alive, and better than ever.
And I know, i owe it all to you.
And all that you to do.
For you there at my lowest, I'm eternally grateful.
Yeah, God sent me my Guardian Angel

Lagged Out

Yeah, life is tough, can feel like one big joke.
To ease the pain, you'd grab one quick smoke.
One becomes many of that there's no doubt.
Now you can't think straight cos' you're feelin' lagged out.

A loved one just passed and you're feeling down.
Like kings & queens when they lose their crown.
When your friend pulls out their bag of green
For the first time in your life, you feel keen.
They offer you one quick puff; little did
they know that wasn't enough.
So, you go ahead and take one big drag, POW!
Brain is fried now you're feeling lagged out.

The weekend has arrived and you're ready for a nice break.
Wanting to hit the clubs, listen to some Em and Aitch.
Work has you exhausted, got ya feelin' dead stiff,
Same friend approaches, askin' "do you wanna sniff?"
If your parents found out they'd scream and shout.
But you don't care, cos' you wanna feel lagged out.

Summer has arrived and you can't wait to go.
Mates invited you to Greece and you couldn't say no,
Touch down in Zante and it's a gorgeous day.
At a boat party and someone offers you K,
Old you would've walked but now you're happy to pay.
Leaving the bathroom, quickly hit the deck.
Yeah, your life was cut short now,
All because you craved the feeling of being lagged out.

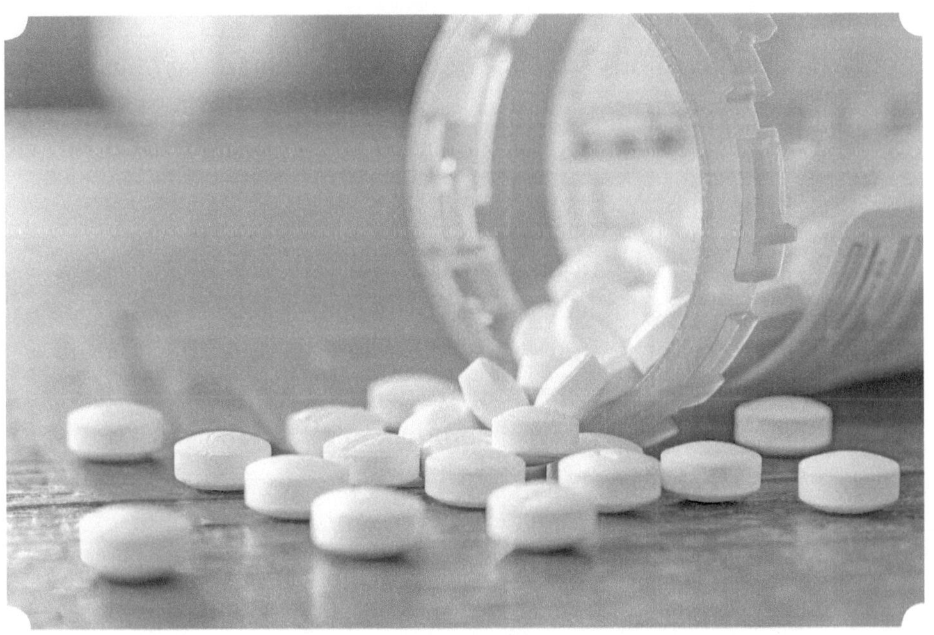

Man of Steel

December is the month of Christmas.
The time for joy, with memories that last forever.
But for a lot of us, this month is a bad omen.
As December is the month we never want to remember.

To your kids and grandkids, you were the Big Strong Man
And that will never change.
Even though we lost you, you're in a better place.
You will always be our Superman.

It was a year and five days apart,
Now there's another massive hole in our hearts.
Hard to find the words to say how I feel.
Last year we lost your wife, my nan, our Nightingale.
Now we've lost you, father, brother, uncle, Grandad, Our
man of steel.

One in the same

3 kids, same father different mother and that's not a sin.
The oldest of the 3 has darker skin.
As her mother was of African descent
Classmates ridiculing her, feeling like she must repent.

Grew up in a house of low income.
He waited patiently for the money to come.
Finally feeling like, in society he does belong.
But co-workers from well off backgrounds have him thinking he's wrong.

People out here, battling the voices in their head.
Their peers saying they're unstable and would be better off dead.
Whether it be schizophrenia or anxiety
Feeling incompetent and alone, daily, and nightly.

It doesn't matter how much you have now or had back then.
Your race, religion, illness, or sexual orientation
You shouldn't make them feel small or take aim.
As we are all human, we're one in the same.

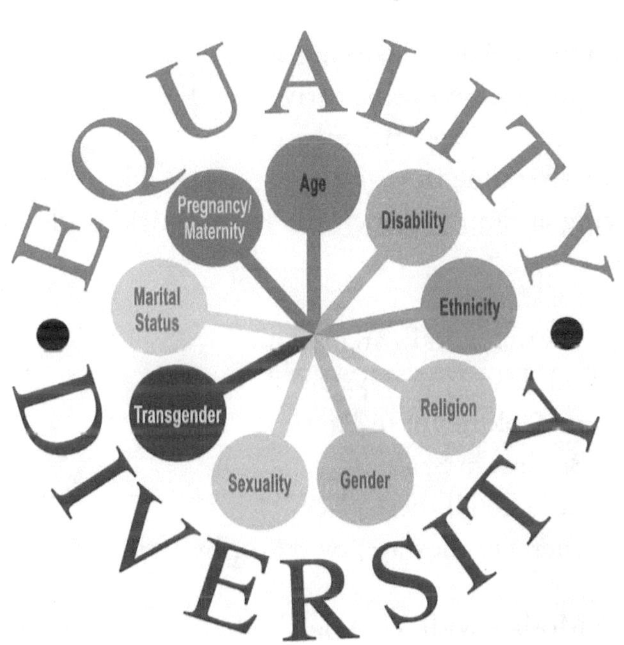

EQUALITY
DIVERSITY
Pregnancy/
Maternity
Age
Disability
Marital
Status
Ethnicity
Transgender
Religion
Sexuality
Gender

Picture Perfect Prophecy

In on the weekdays, working a 9-5.
Weekends off, on this he thrives.
This meant he had Christmas off.
For the first time in years
Arriving at family dinner, the room quickly filled with
cheers.

They visit the world's architecture.
With both history and beauty
From the Colosseum in Rome
to the Basilica in Spain
They could go all these places.
From wherever they are, by bus or by train.

Single Mother with 3 young children
House in a mess, she's under immense stress.
To calm the situation, she would tell each.
To quickly get ready, were going to the beach.
Her car, she wouldn't need to load.
For at the back of their humble abode
was a place where her kids can have hours of fun.
And she can soak up the sun.

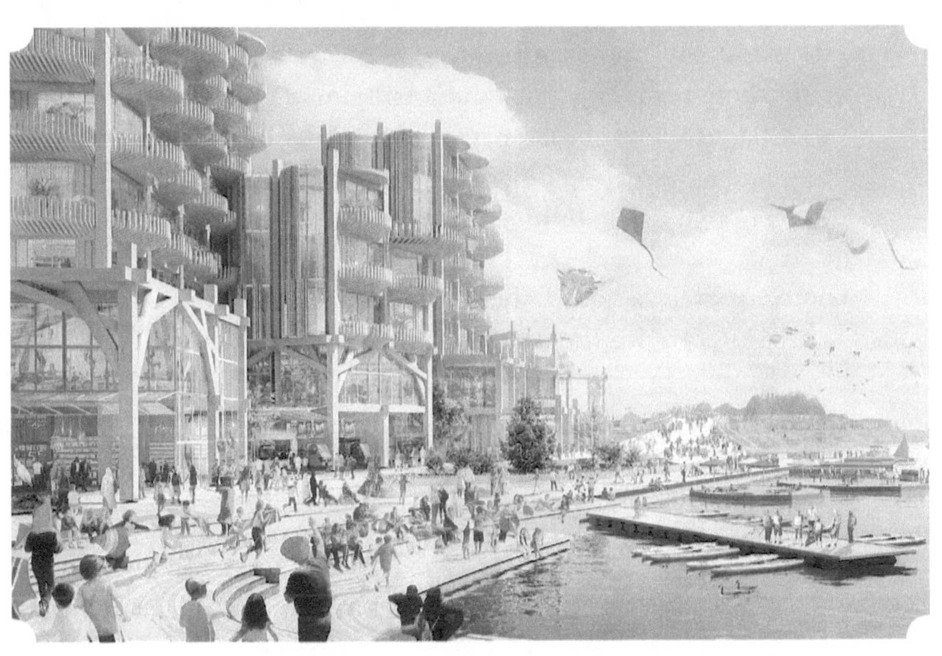

Pint Sized Angel

The world was ready, for you to grace it with your presence
But those plans changed, and it still doesn't make sense
Ella was your chosen name, enchanting by nature
The new year was meant to bring a new chapter
You were never held but hearts you still managed to capture

You were to have your father's smile and your mother's eyes
But it's with the latter that they constantly cry
4 weeks premature, as small as a dainty butterfly
To the big guy up there, they're eternally disdainful
Taken way to soon, you pint sized angel.

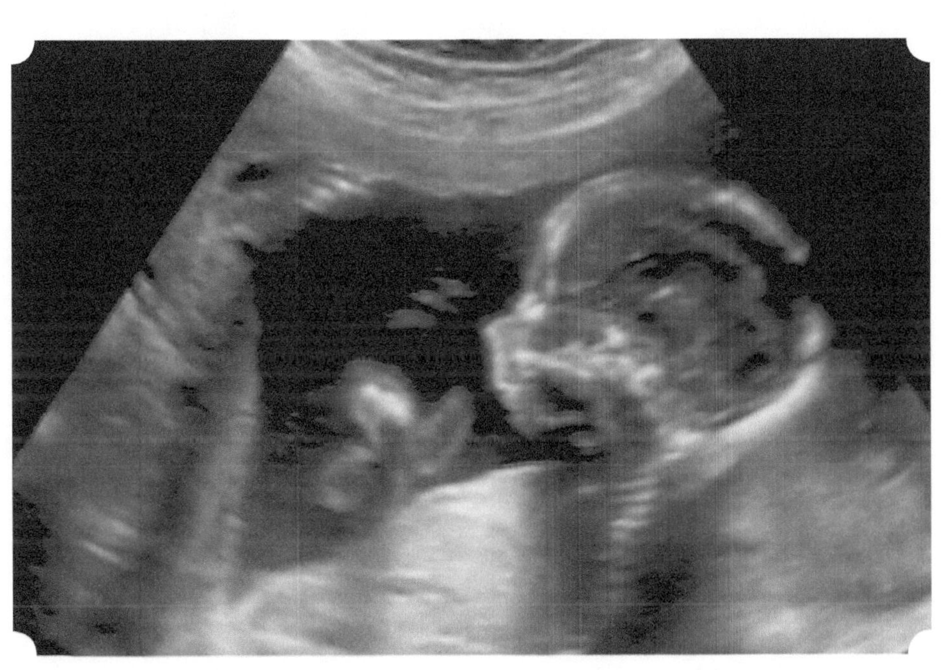

Rite of Passage

Hopping from job to job, and it makes you wonder.
Good at what you were asked to do, so why
do they treat you like a number.
Applying again, needed to give positive
feedback, of which they would.
Companies are all about money, that you understood.

Exams are around the corner and you're stressing out.
Studied hard but fearing failure, of that there's no doubt.
Even if you do manage to succeed.
Will you get the points that you need?

But look at you know; you proved the doubters wrong.
With your family and high paying job,
you never felt this headstrong.
You are a product of your own device.
Don't be afraid to gamble and roll your dice.

Life is filled with ups and downs.
When it comes to employment, many do their rounds.
Everybody has a purpose, whether they're aware or not.
If you're interested in something, just give it a shot.
This is not an order, but it is a message.
Take the risk, for it could be your rite of passage.

Stick to your roots.

Family is the glue that will always hold onto you.
Whether they are near or far.
No matter how old you are.
never be ashamed, to stick to your roots.

Fiancé just dipped, feeling like your heart has been ripped.
Contrary to what you may believe, they'll always understand.
When you need a lift, they'll offer their hands.
It's not too late, to stick to your roots.

6 years have gone by, and all you can do is cry.
You and your new partner just welcomed child number four.
Happier know then you've ever been before.
Be there for your loved ones, not just whenever it suits.
Life is better now, for you decided to stick to your roots.

Like a Swan to Cold Water

She's always happy no matter the weather,
That smile on her face makes my day much better.
She'll smile at anything, it's really no bother.
Yeah, that girl is like a swan to cold water.

She'll watch any movie, there's never a fuss.
Having a woman like her is a real must,
She's open to having kids, dreams of a daughter.
Yeah, that girl is like a swan to cold water.

I listen to everything, but she isn't fazed
When she caught my eye, it was the happiest of days.
She has loads of friends, not one ever fought her.
Yeah, that girl is like a swan to cold water.

Down by the dock we fish every week
With her by my side, life is never bleak
She was my catch of the day, and it's lasted a lifetime.
With the proof being the diamond ring that I bought her.
For she is my everything, she's like a swan to cold water.

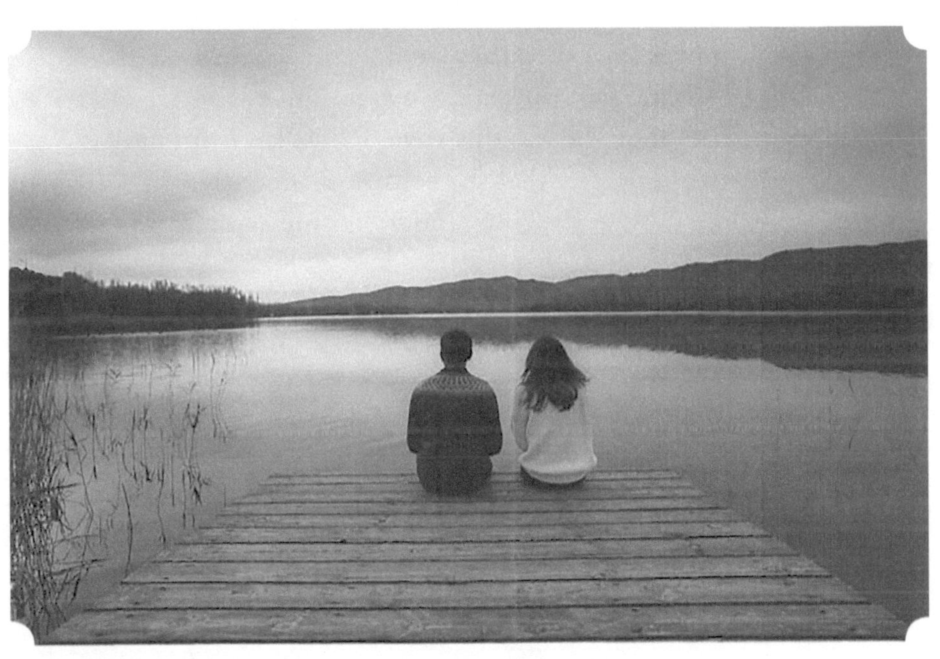

Galaxies Apart

Yeah, I never imagined that she'd seem Galaxies Apart
She first caught my eye in 2011,
My immediate thought was this angel had fallen from heaven.
Wasn't long after that she became a close friend
But sadly, like most at the time, the friendship came to an end.

There was not one fight that we ever had,
We were just 2 individuals, each with a different path.
Circumstances dictate the path that you pave
Unfortunately, my path couldn't be saved.
Spent the rest of the year in my bedroom at home.
With no friends to turn to, I was all alone.

I went for walks when I felt more mellow,
Time to time I'd see her and stop to say hello.
She has a boyfriend now, he has won her heart
She's really happy, he's clearly doing his part.

If she was ever insulted, I'd defend her to no end
Little did she know, I wasn't always doing it as a friend.
But I never had the words, no clue where to start,
Now it's too late, as we are Galaxies Apart.

Man's Best Friend

His name was Pip, and he was a mini yorkie,
My favourite gift brought countless amazing memories.
We were inseparable, he went everywhere with me.

If he heard a loud noise, he'd run to my bedside,
He'd scratch and bark, give me the puppy dog eyes.
He wouldn't go back downstairs as he was too scared,
On nights like these it was my bed that we shared.

So, imagine my shock, on the day I graduate
That I return home to no sign of my best mate.
He ran out the door as my parents packed the car,
He wound up in Finglas, he made it pretty far.

Last I heard he was living with an elderly pair,
All I could think was 'this isn't fair'.
At the time it was the toughest parting that I had faced,
Man's best friend, you'll never be replaced.

Nightingale

God gained an angel, as the year came to a close,
All our hearts, over they froze.
December was when you passed,
Your life, forever I prayed it would last.
When I got the news I dropped to my knees,
The only solace we have is you're finally at peace.

Still the months, they float by like years,
As we all continue to drown in a river of tears.
The days seem longer, the nights are feeling colder.
We'll miss you nan, as we all get older,
You are the nightingale, perched forever atop our shoulders.

Shadow Boxer

Everybody believes they're going 10 months strong,
Nobody would imagine that something was wrong.
Not even her family had a clue,
That when he arrived home from work, he left her black and blue.

Ashamed to show his true colours,
Afraid to tell her older brothers.
He acts like a saint when the attention is on her,
But lashes out behind closed doors, call him a shadow boxer.

He came home early, and she had packed her stuff.
With her brother by her side, crying out 'I've had enough'.
She's moved on now and found the perfect guy.
With him in her life the only tears she cries, is those of joy.

As for her ex, he's in a bit of a rut.
Karma has hit and the shoes on the other foot.
She is much stronger than he, afraid to lay a finger on her.
He now knows it feels, to live with a shadow boxer.

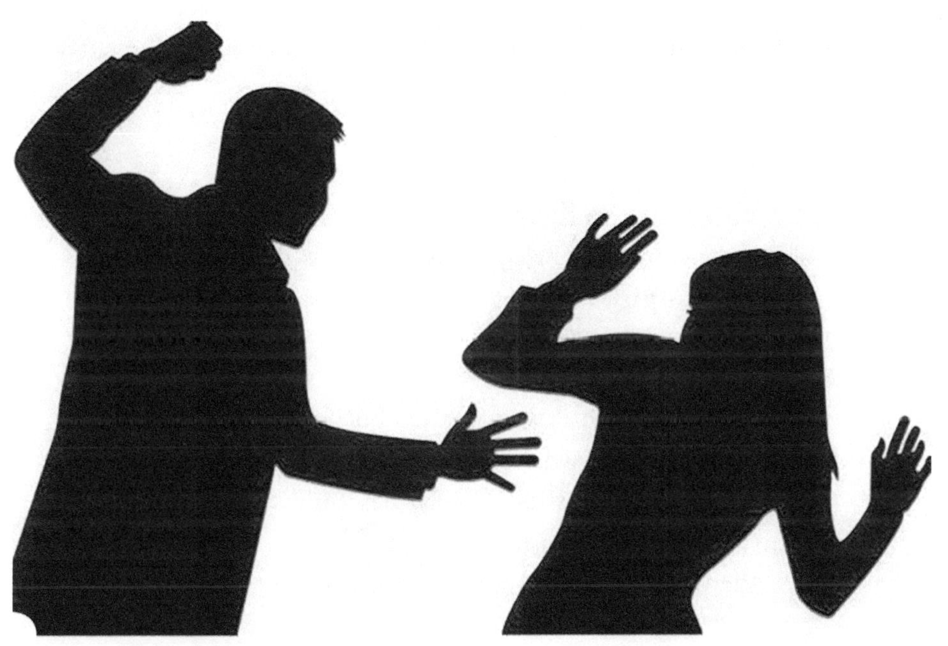

Silent Camera

We all know that memories can last forever
Praying for some to leave you never
A child has been born
In the early hours of the morn
With a smile on their face that lights up the room
The parents were overjoyed, with words you'd assume
It was girl, had no idea what to name her.
Both with nothing to say, not even how to describe her.

A picture it speaks a thousand words, but for this we had none
Standing behind their classmates with their fingers imitating a gun.
It could've been harmless, everyone could've been fine,
But the picture in question was the students of Columbine.
Pictures, whether ingrained or on paper, can
be precious and that's the truth,
But there is also many that will leave us all mute.

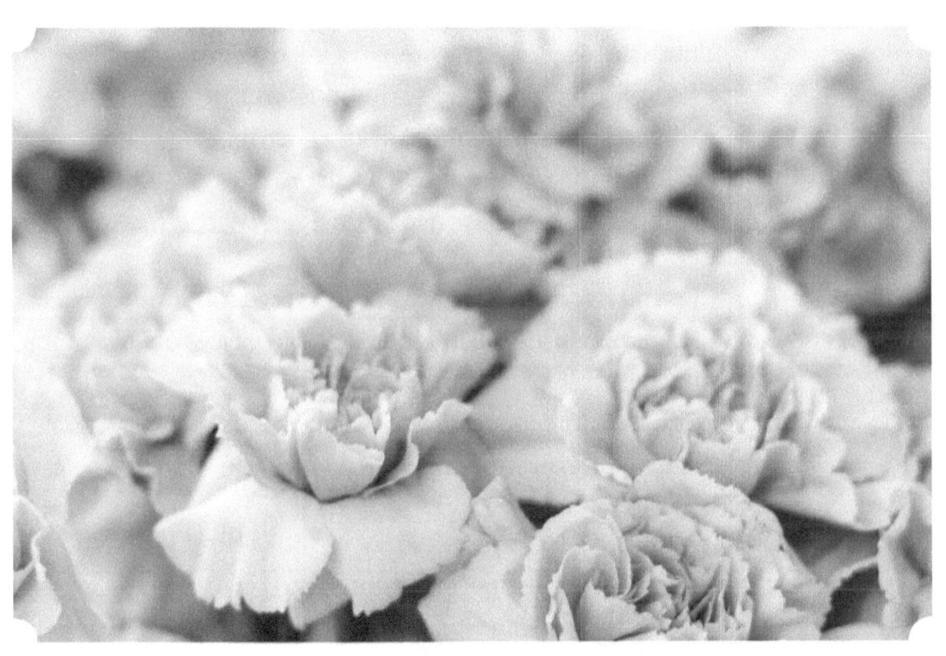

Driven by the Hate

There's always a cheap remark to make
Whether I show up 5 minutes early or 15 minutes late.
Just keep the comments coming, because
I'm not flustered by the slate.
See, what you don't realise is that I'm driven by the hate.

Picking away when I was at my lowest
I had a different mindset then and man I know it
Still bothered, but no longer need to show it.
Laugh all you want, that I haven't had my first date.
Because little do you know, I'm driven by the hate.

I know I'm not the only one to experience something like this,
Sick and tired of people taking the piss
Only you can decide your fate
Please, use the comments as motivation,
So, you too can become, driven by the hate.

A Rose With no Thorns

Beautiful to the human eye
Like the early autumn sky
Precious as a secret that lasts forever
Wishing it could stay, never say never
As rare as a blue moon
Or even a quiet afternoon
Red as the heart
Of loved ones here, and those who depart
As ingrained in your head
As the day your child was born
For you have not seen true beauty
Until you see a rose with no thorns.

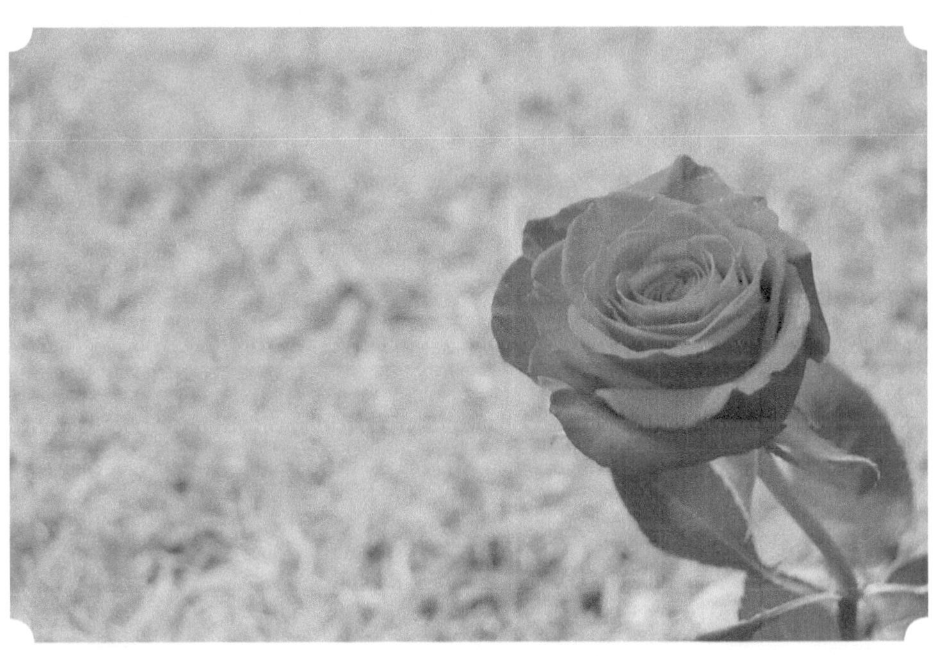

Cheetah Print

You found the girl of your dreams
And it's still hard to believe
Life is filled with accomplishments
This being one of the toughest for many to achieve
You always feared that it would be one quick stint
For saw her at the beach, rocking the cheetah print

1 year anniversary yeah, she truly is the best
You love your watches, so she bought you a Rolex
Walking past Louis Vuitton, and something catches your eye
It's the bag she's wanted for months, you just had to buy.
The bag had a familiar tint, as she'd soon
be styling in cheetah print.

2 years married, with 2 beautiful girls
So, you are in shock by how quick it unfurls
The signs were there, blinded by love you ignored every hint
She had left you nothing, but a broken heart and a cheetah print.

Trend Setter

It's a Saturday night, and you don't feel right
Had a relationship ending row with your
love, leaving you both miserable
You feel it more as you're softer and that's just typical.

A few familiar faces walk into the club
One of these used to be your plug.
They see you alone and they're all asking why
While you're holding by the emotions, trying not to cry.

They stay with you the rest of the night
And they've got your back
They support you as they say
"we'll get you back on track"

The time is flying and so are the drinks
Plug offers you white, only one that said no
Even though you're on the brink.
You never gave into the peer pressure,
Building yourself up, who walked away and became
Your own trend setter.

Laws and Outlaws

A bunch of people came together for a tourney of Madden
Nobody could've foreseen what was about to happen
Good Luck Have Fun was the name of the bar
Far from the case, as it would leave families with a permanent scar
We all know the phrase "sore loser"
This man takes the cake, but he also a misuser
After losing, he returns to the venue to fire off 12 shots
It most the most unexpected of onslaughts
Ten were injured by the scattered shells
Sadly, two were killed, the third victim
he turned the gun on himself.

64-year-old man on the Las Vegas Strip
From what we know, nobody gave him lip
Officially undetermined remains the motive
This man would leave hundreds of families forever votive.
Unleashed more than 1,000 bullets,
wounded 400 and 60 were killed.
And when he was found by police it was
his own blood that he spilled.

On his 18th birthday he decided to purchase
2 firearms, an AR and a handgun
Returning home to his grandma he used
one her, but sadly he wasn't done.
Robb Elementary was his next location
And like the movies, it would be his Final Destination
Walked past an officer wielding the assault rifle
Yet for some reason the office wasn't stifled
This monster killed 2 teachers and 19 students, kid after kid
Taken were their lives, as well as their families farewells to bid

It's scary, you had 656 mass shootings last
year, according to the GVA
With 40,000 firearm related deaths, yet you have nothing to say.
I'm begging you, please introduce some stricter laws
That way you can prolong and hopefully stop
Some of the crazed outlaws.

Steal a life away!

She was a teenage girl on her way to school.
Why did this young boy have to be so cruel?
Whole life ahead of her, could've amounted to many things in life.
But she never got that opportunity for it was taken with a knife.

Small innocent child out shopping with his mother.
This day should've been like any other.
When she let go of his hand, she would be left to wallow.
As two young boys took his hand and
hours later his life would follow.

Young woman walking home after a late shift.
Nice looking couple pull over, asking if she wants a lift.
As she was tired, she accepted with glee.
But little did she know this couple were
the most evil you could see.
Took many a life including their own spawn.
Down infamously in history these two have gone.

Nurse was her profession and trusted, was she.
But she had cruel intentions, and to carry them out she was free.
Young children were passing out unexpectedly.
She took seven lives, the other six got very lucky.

Many look back on these, case after case.
Coming to the realisation that the world really is a scary place.
For when we hear things like this, we all want to say.
Why would they want, to steal a life away?

Castle in the Sky

Unable to get all those feelings off your chest
One misdiagnosis and your partner was laid to rest.
Your mates flew to Vegas to see the big fight
But their plane disappeared out of sight
Uncle was having another argument with his wife
Unfortunately, this time she would take her own life.

Unknowingly drove you and your fiancé home drunk he did
2 fatalities that could've easily been avoided.
At a gig when someone pulls out a gun, has you thinking twice
Grazes you but hits your sibling, feeling
you've paid the ultimate price.
Best mate is gone, of time you've lost track,
All because had this random girl's back.

Parents are left speechless, forever they will internally cry
Figuring it was way too soon to every say goodbye
Alone in your room, endless tears that you shed
Gone are the times that they'd put you to bed.
They may no longer be visible to the human eye
But they'll always be watching over you,
From that Castle in the Sky.

Body and Choice

Abortion laws, stopped by a male majority
Leaving women the silent minority.
In many instances, their bodies are on the line
Yet at the verdict they were never give the time.

We should all see a problem with this change in life
Guns now have more rights than your
sister, daughter, mother or wife.
Instead of making future advances that are positive
We're going back to the suffragettes, and that's no way to live.

I understand that life is a right
But this decision put women's at risk and that not alright.
Whether it was a result of assault,
or she's too young or poor to provide adequate care
this change is ridiculous, to women it's totally unfair

Embryos are organisms, yet to reach their human form
So, if a woman wishes to abort, they shouldn't be scorned
When this law was being changed, women should've had the voice.
Because at the end of the day, it's their body and their choice.

Dress to Repress

It's a new year at the same old school
But this brought a new principal to enforce new rules.
The rules to teachers, somewhat made sense
But they directly mainly at one sex.

New rules were a dress code, away with the times.
Students alike, how this still applies
Girls accepting, unlike the boys.
As they no longer had somewhere to focus their eyes.

Couple days later, the principal would break some tragic news.
Some female students from the nearest school were assaulted
They were wearing skimpy clothing that night
But everyone agreed, that didn't give those men the right.

Following this event, the boys' behaviour forever changed
There was no more catcalling during class, or inappropriate names
For this change of heart, the old school dress code would bless
As the girls no longer felt they had to dress to repress.

About the Author

Hello, my name is Aaron, I'm 25 years old. I started writing poetry a little over three years ago as a way to deal with heartache and stress. This newfound passion has given me a new outlook on life.

www.ingramcontent.com/pod-product-compliance
Lightning Source LLC
Chambersburg PA
CBHW021347060726
47591CB00006B/2194